Nurse Swear

Beautiful Critters

with Bad Mouths

By

R. Randolph

Copyright © 2016 by R. Randolph

All rights reserved worldwide. No part of this publication may be reproduced or distributed in any form or by any means, mechanical, electronic or stored in a retrieval or database system, without written permission from the copyright holder.

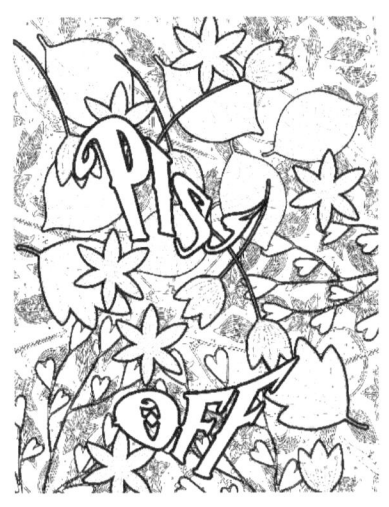

Happy Coloring!

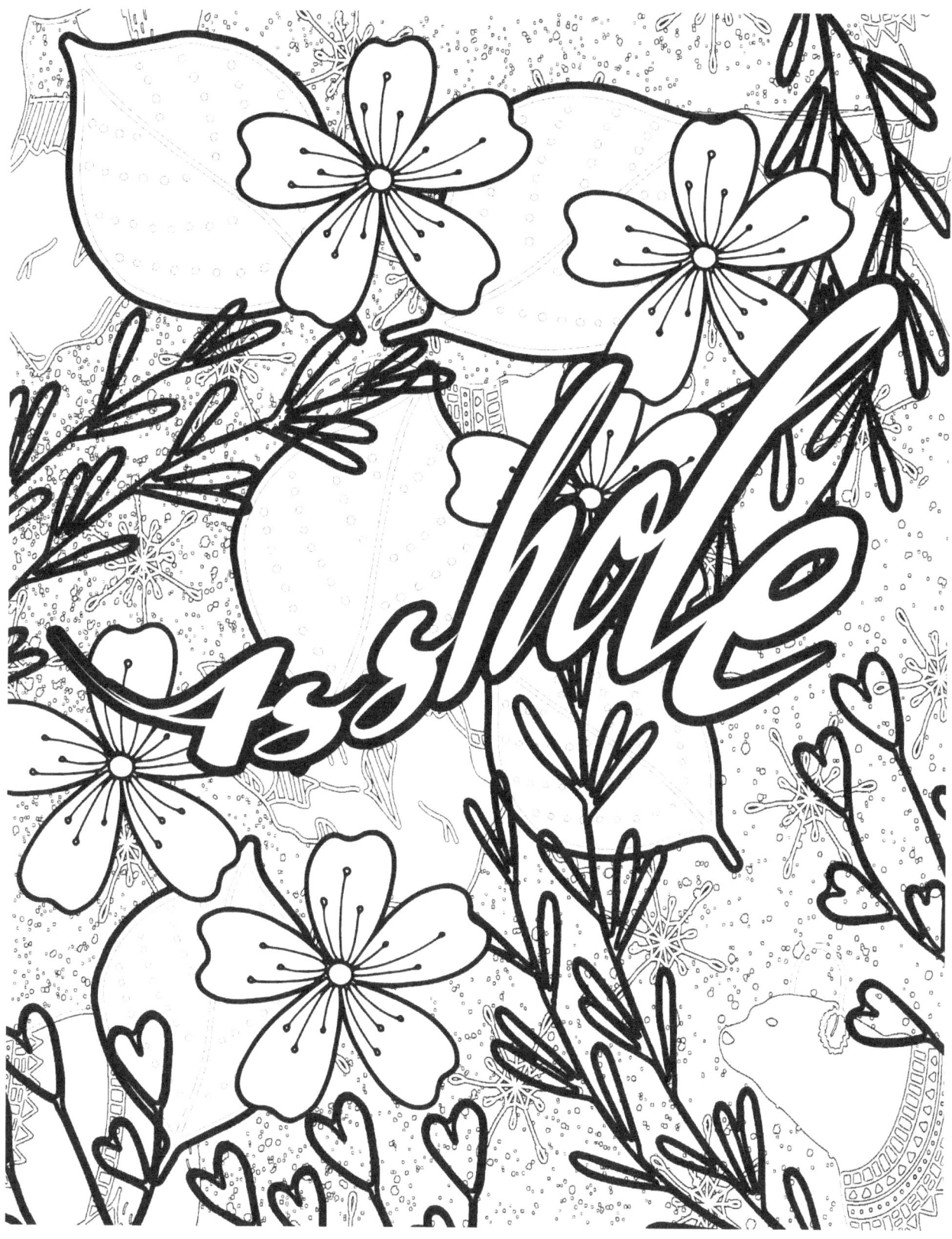

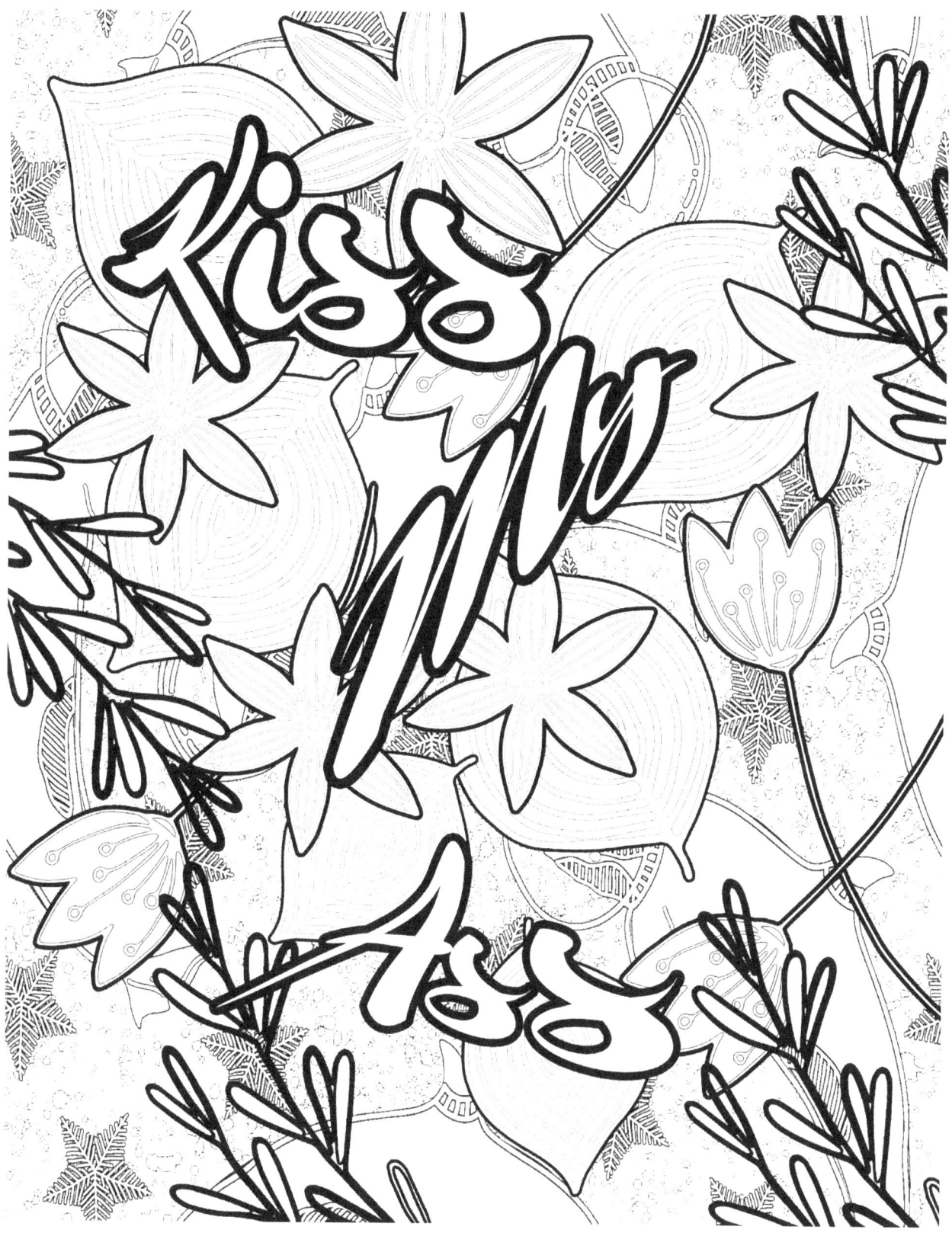

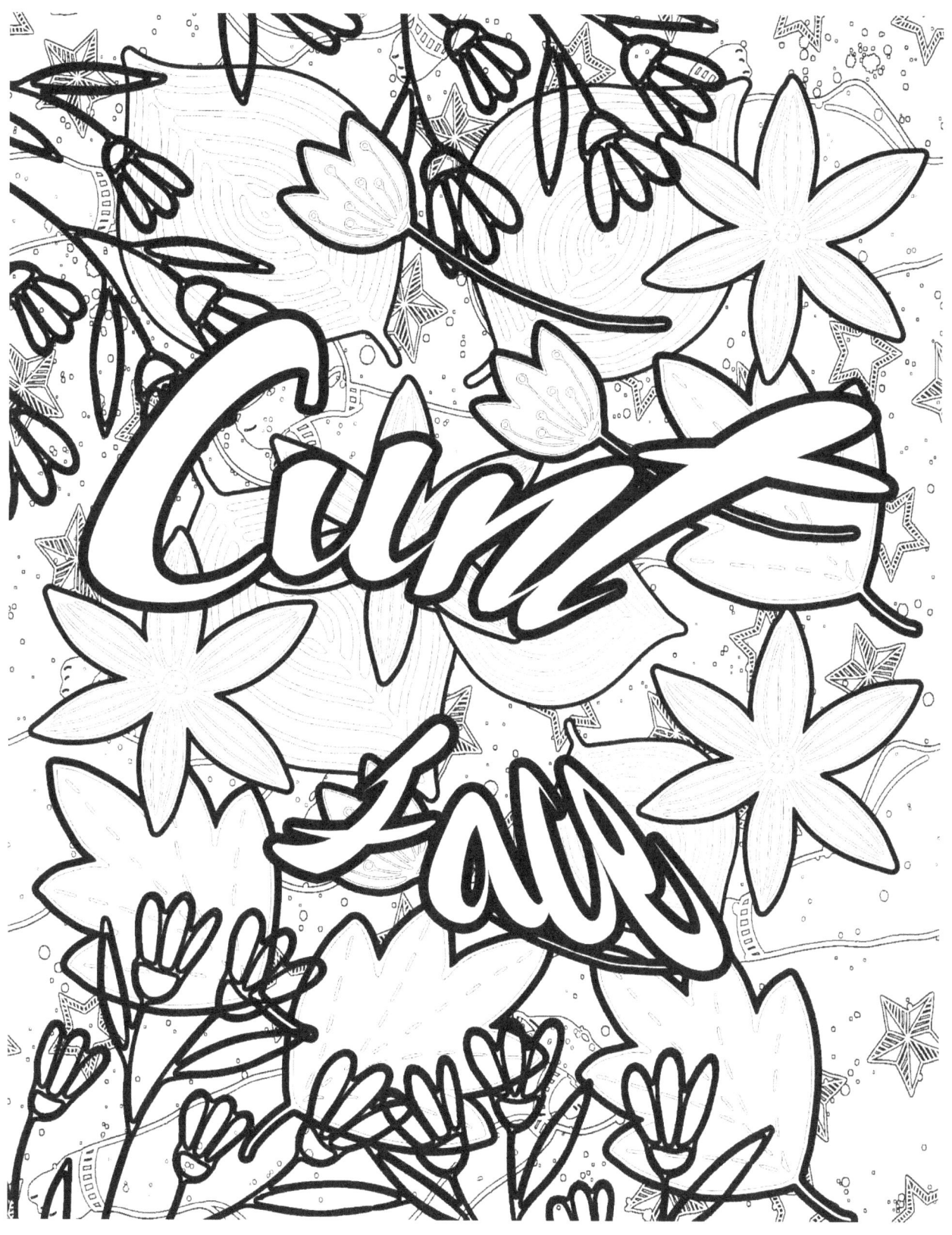

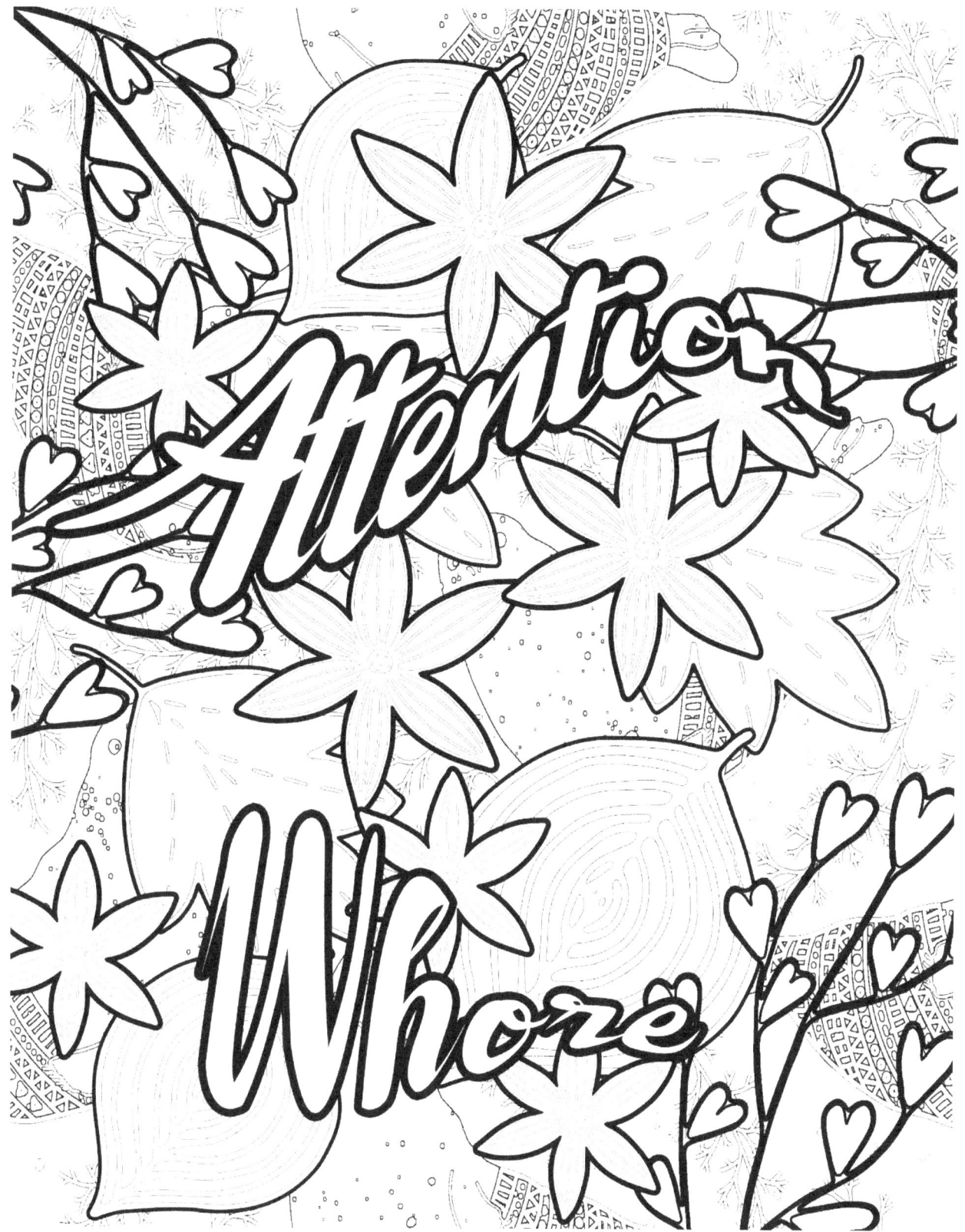

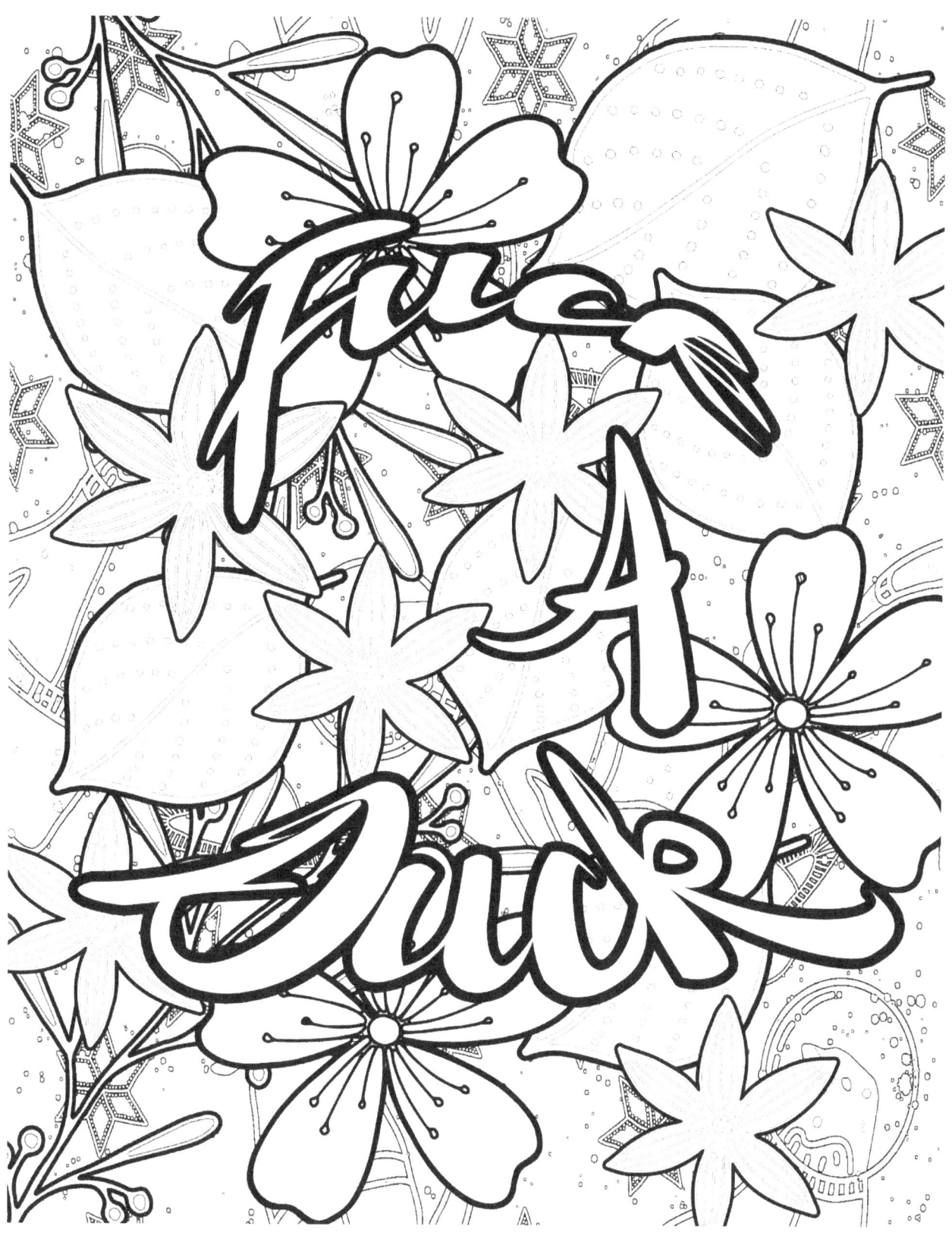

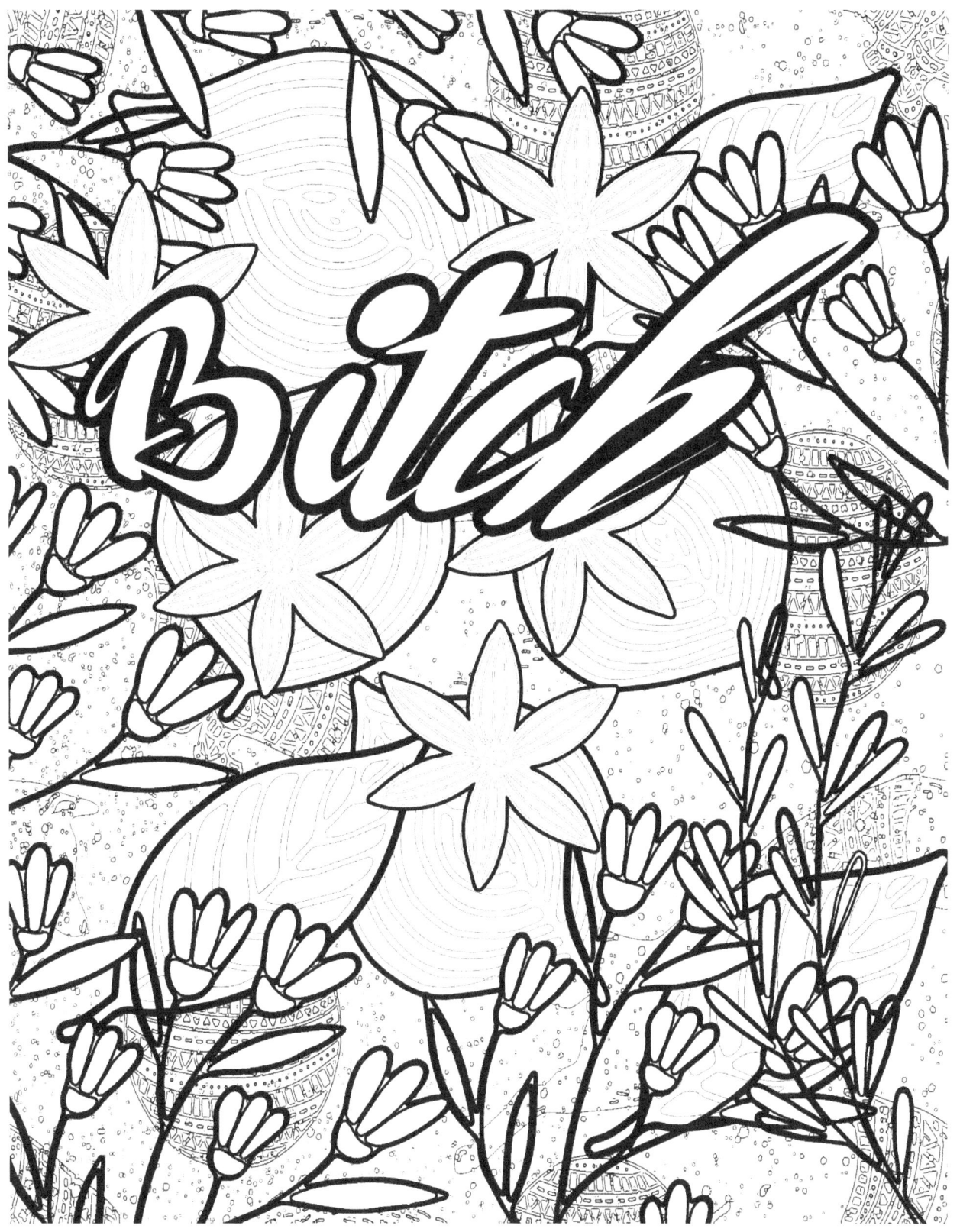

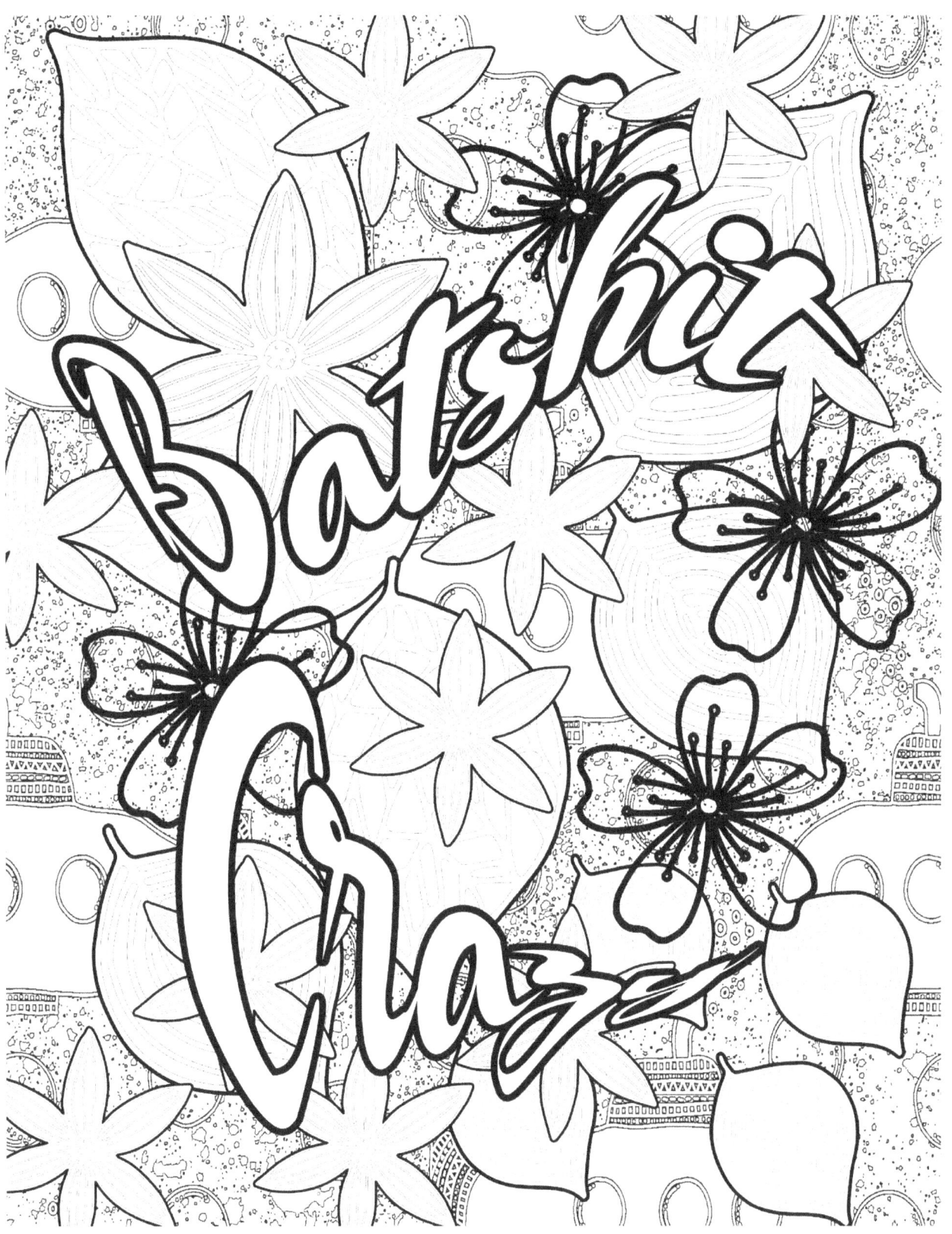

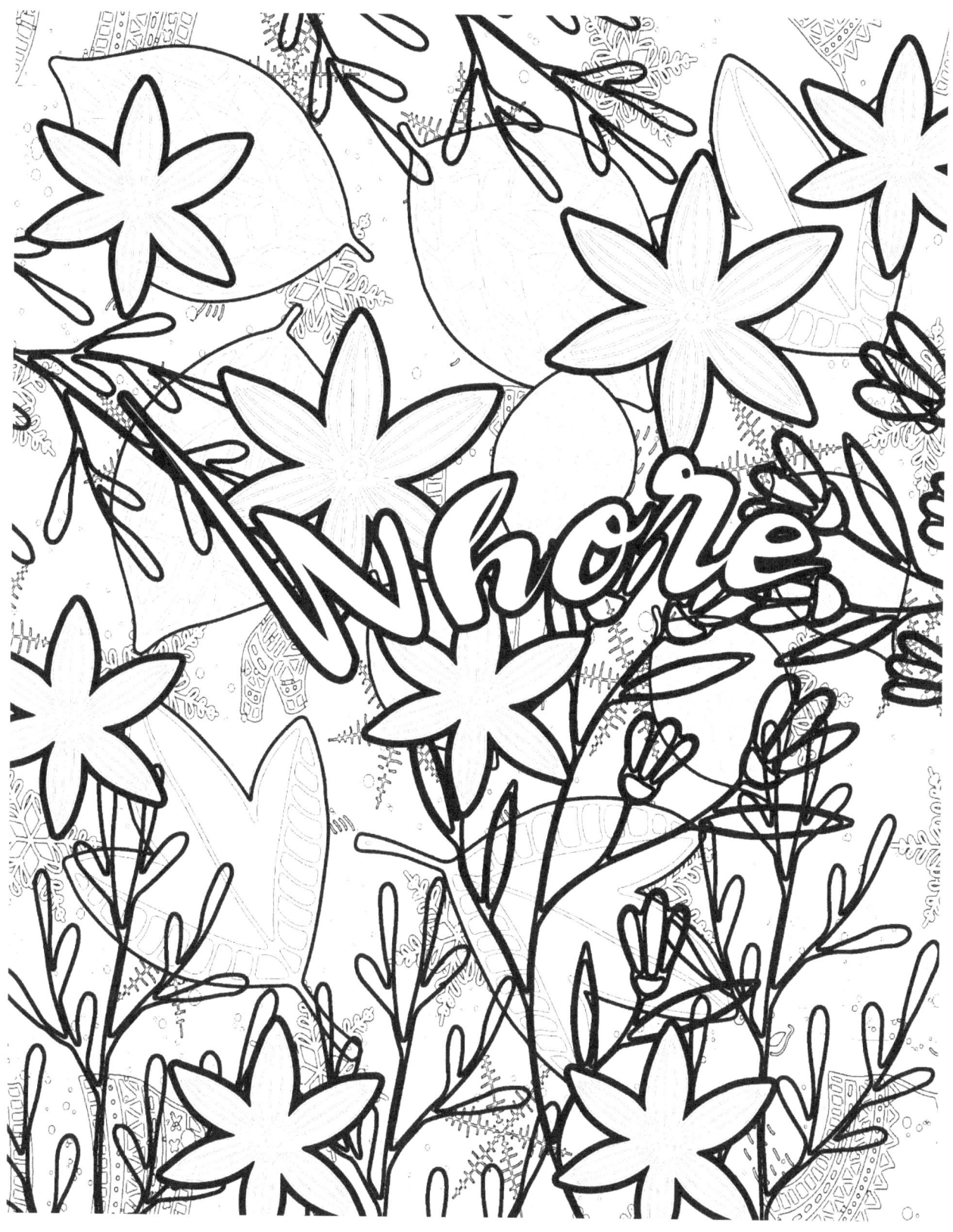

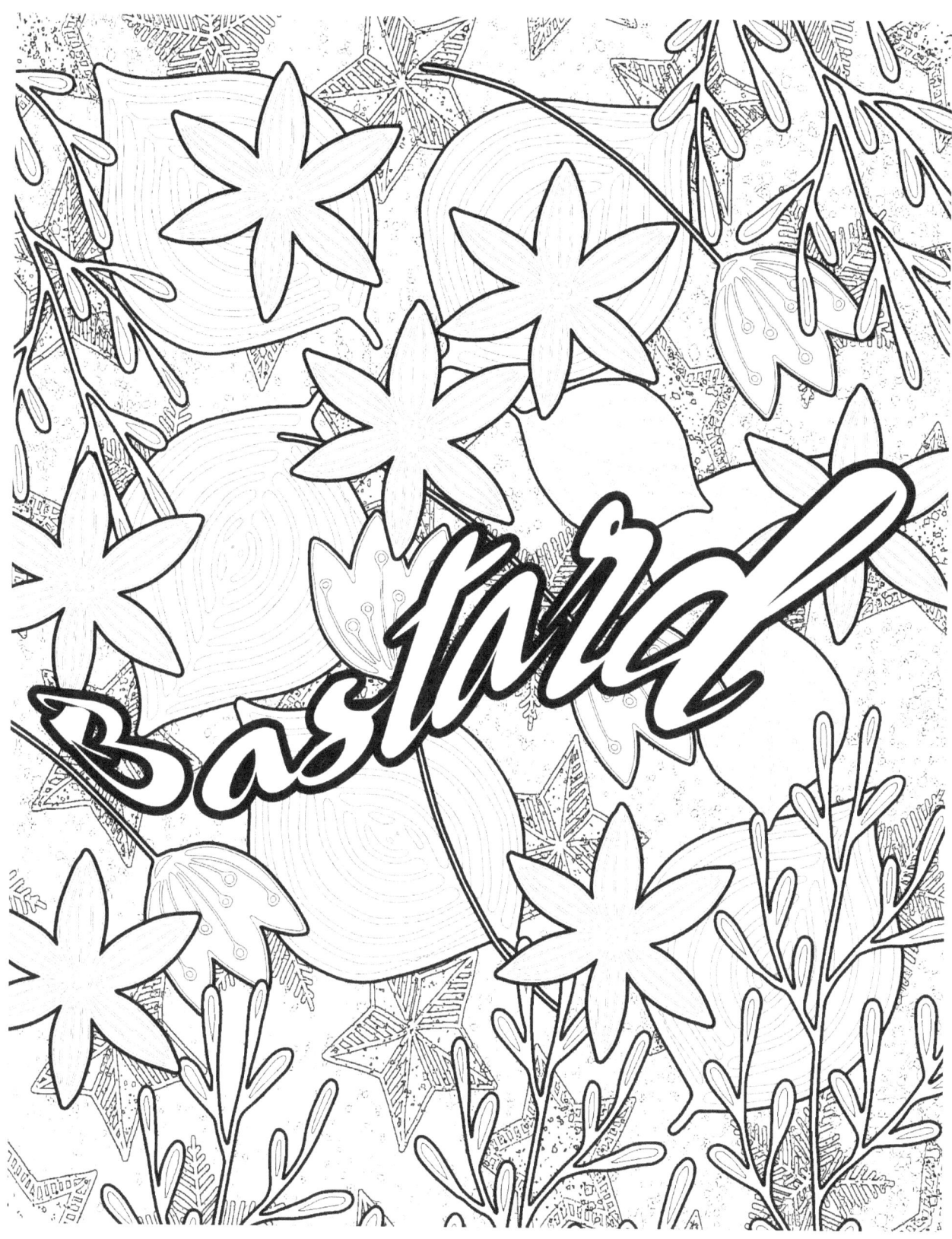

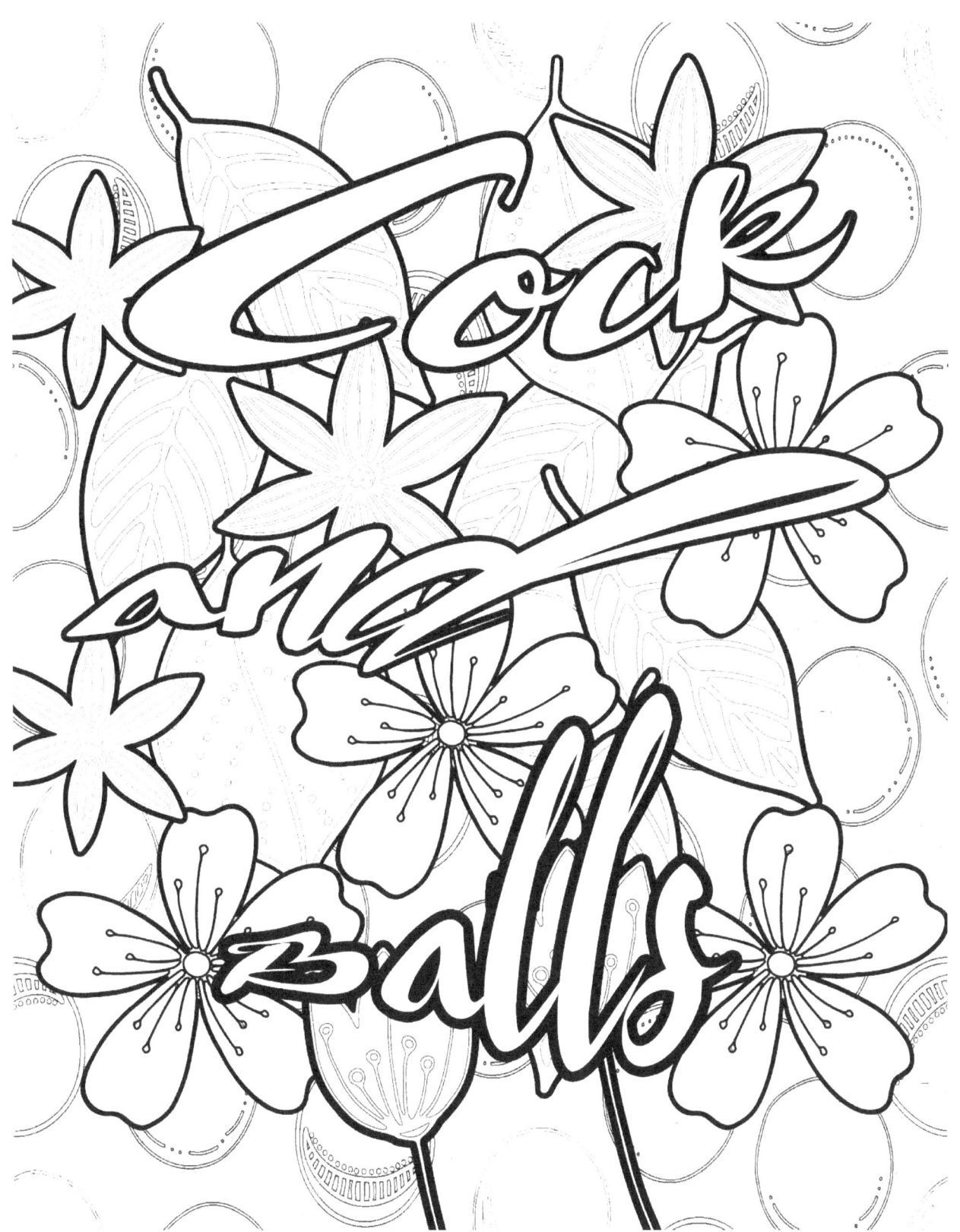

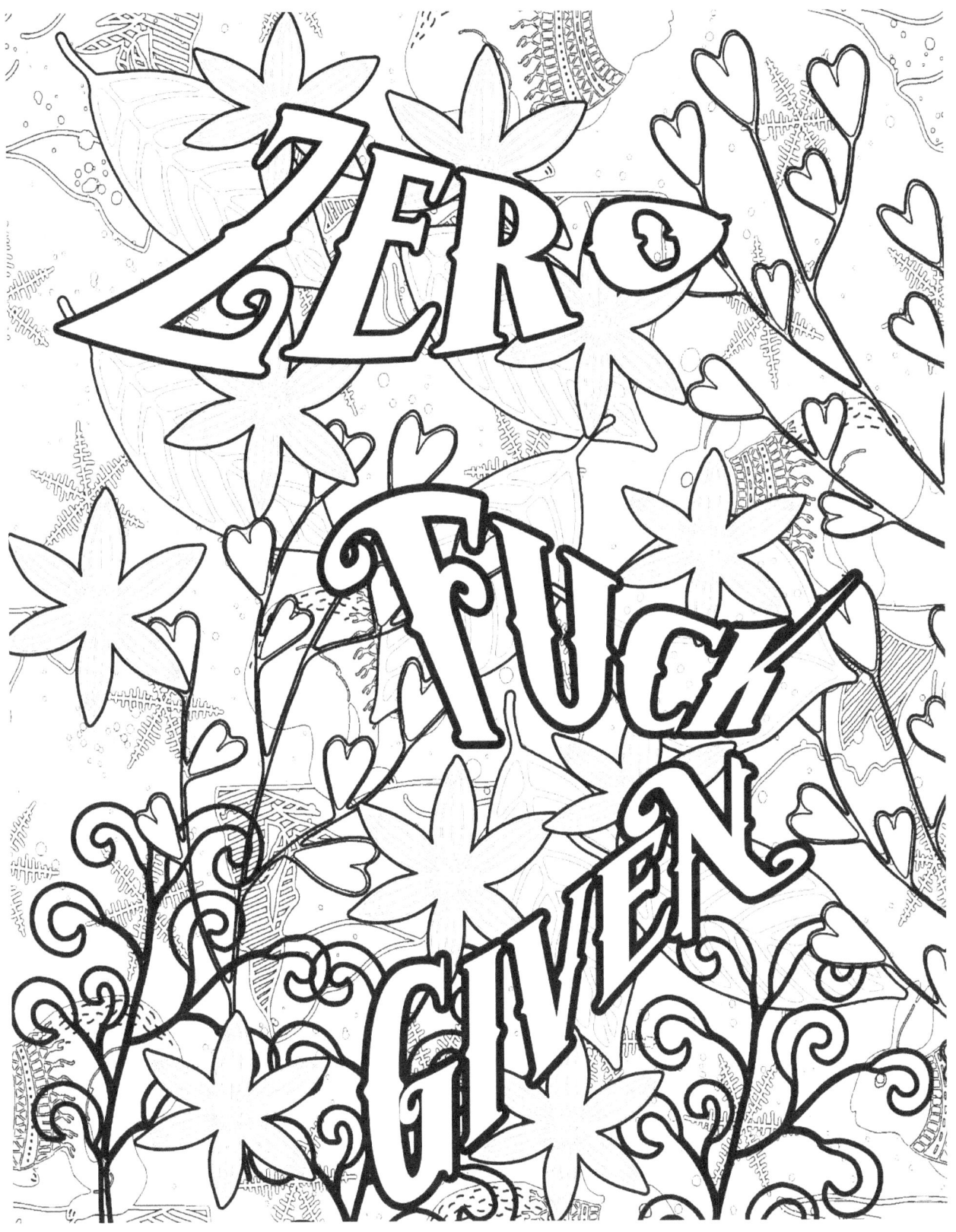

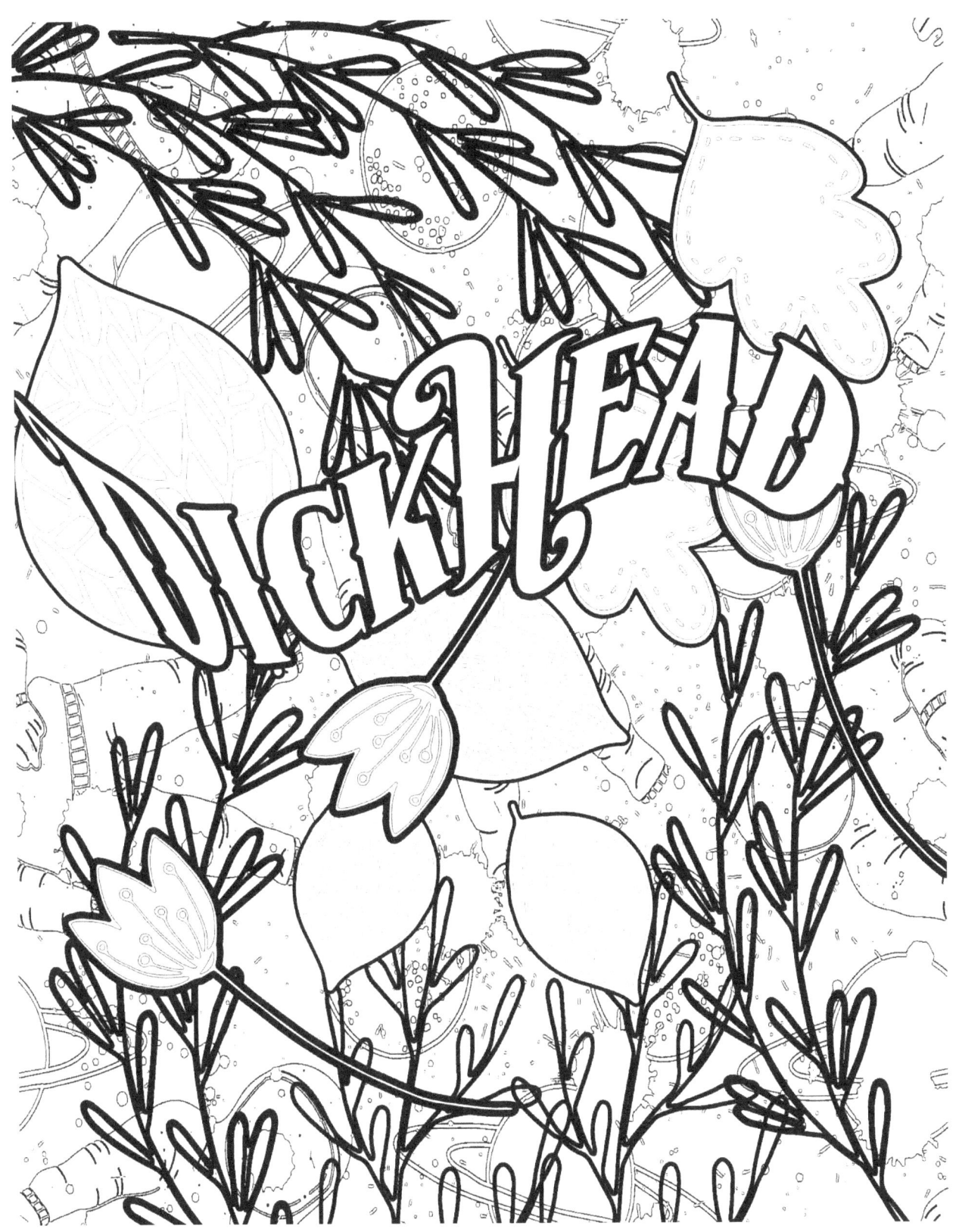

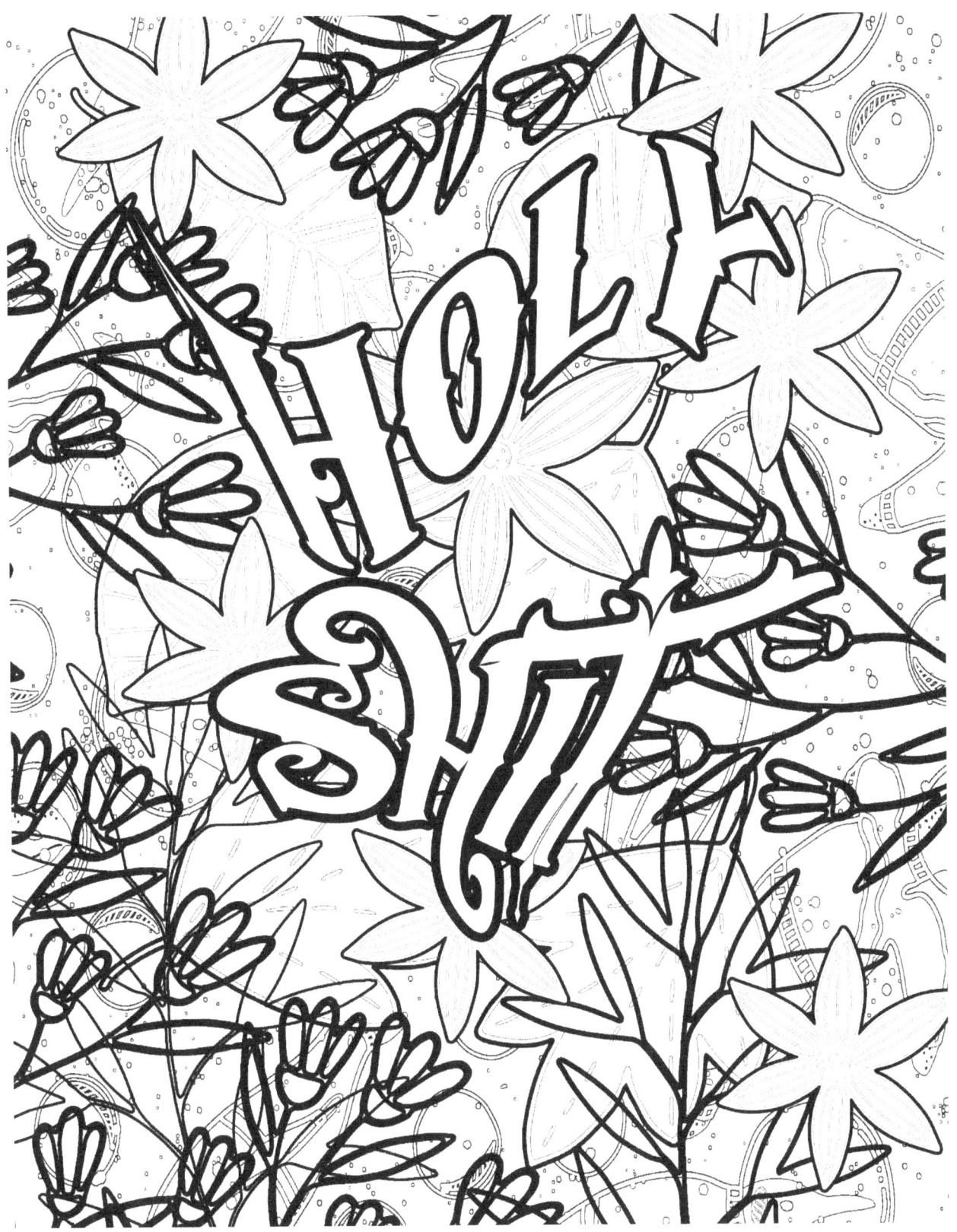

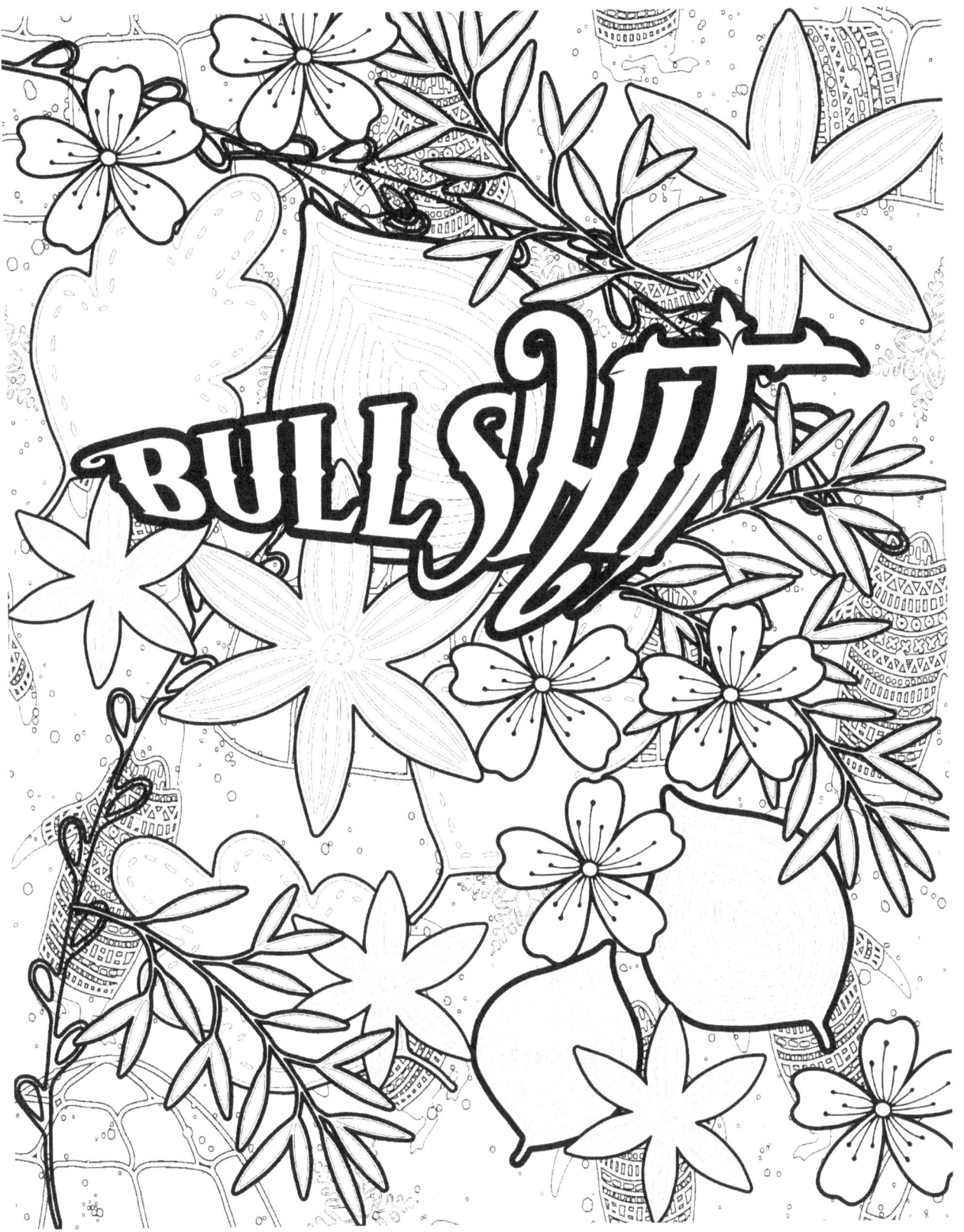

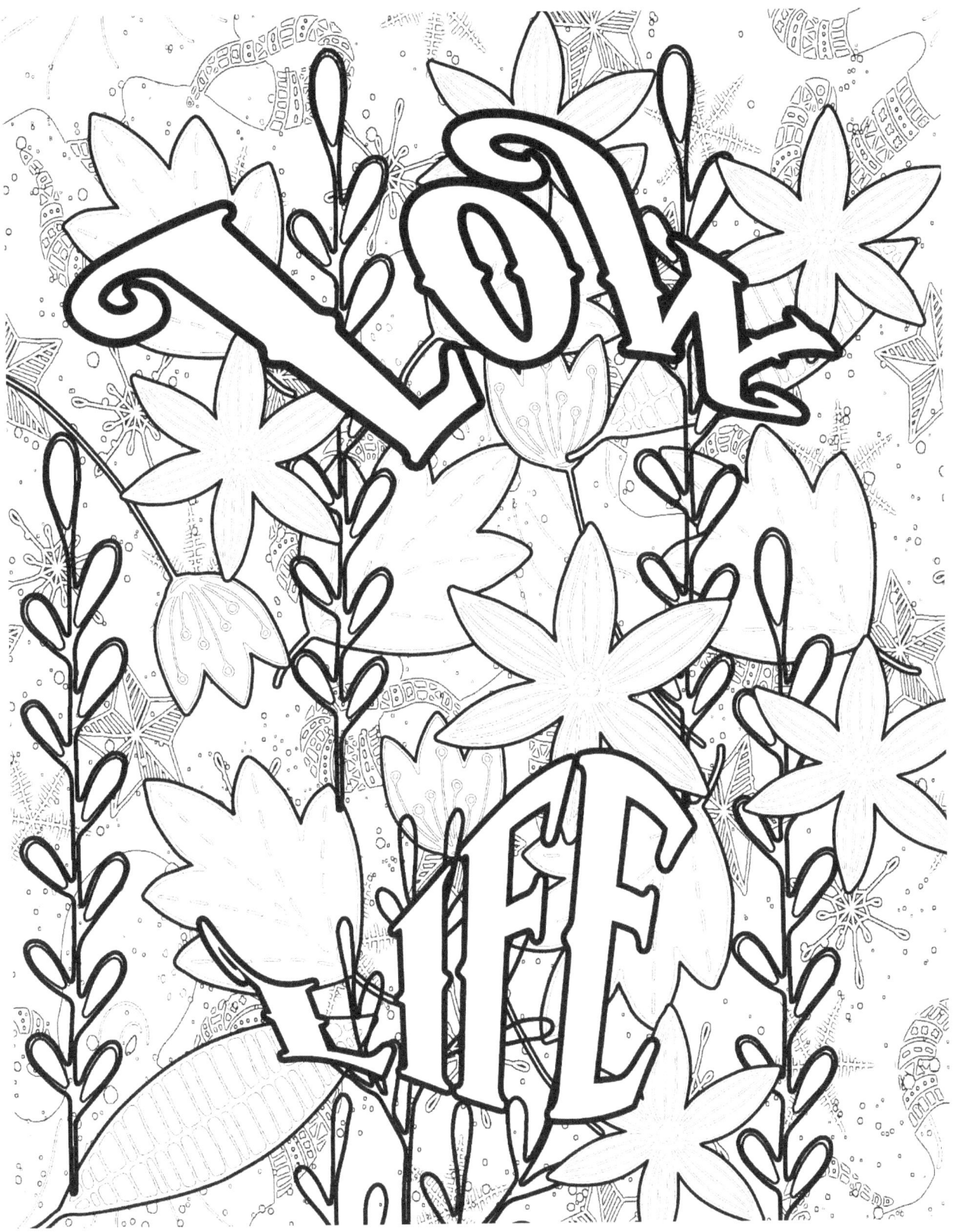

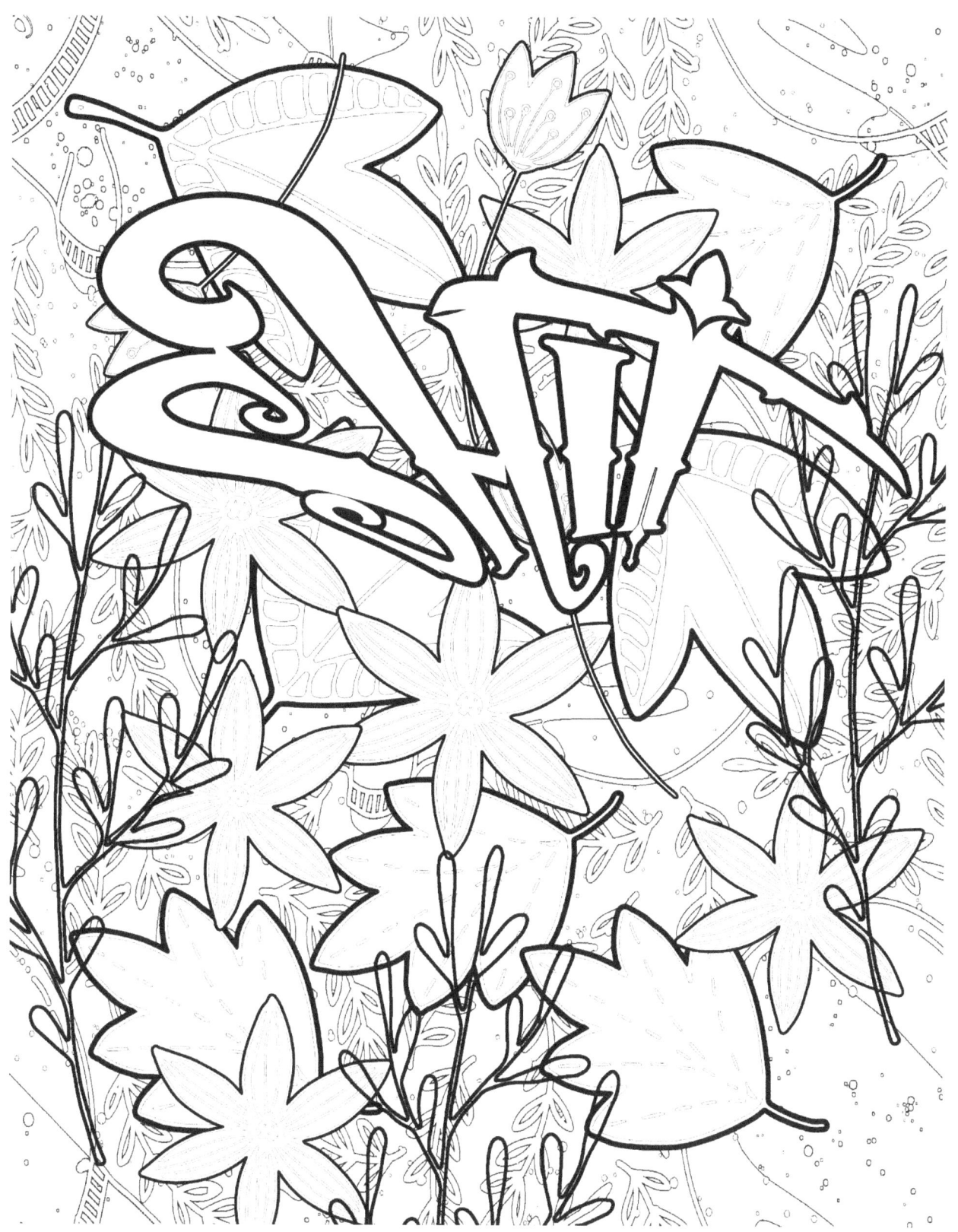

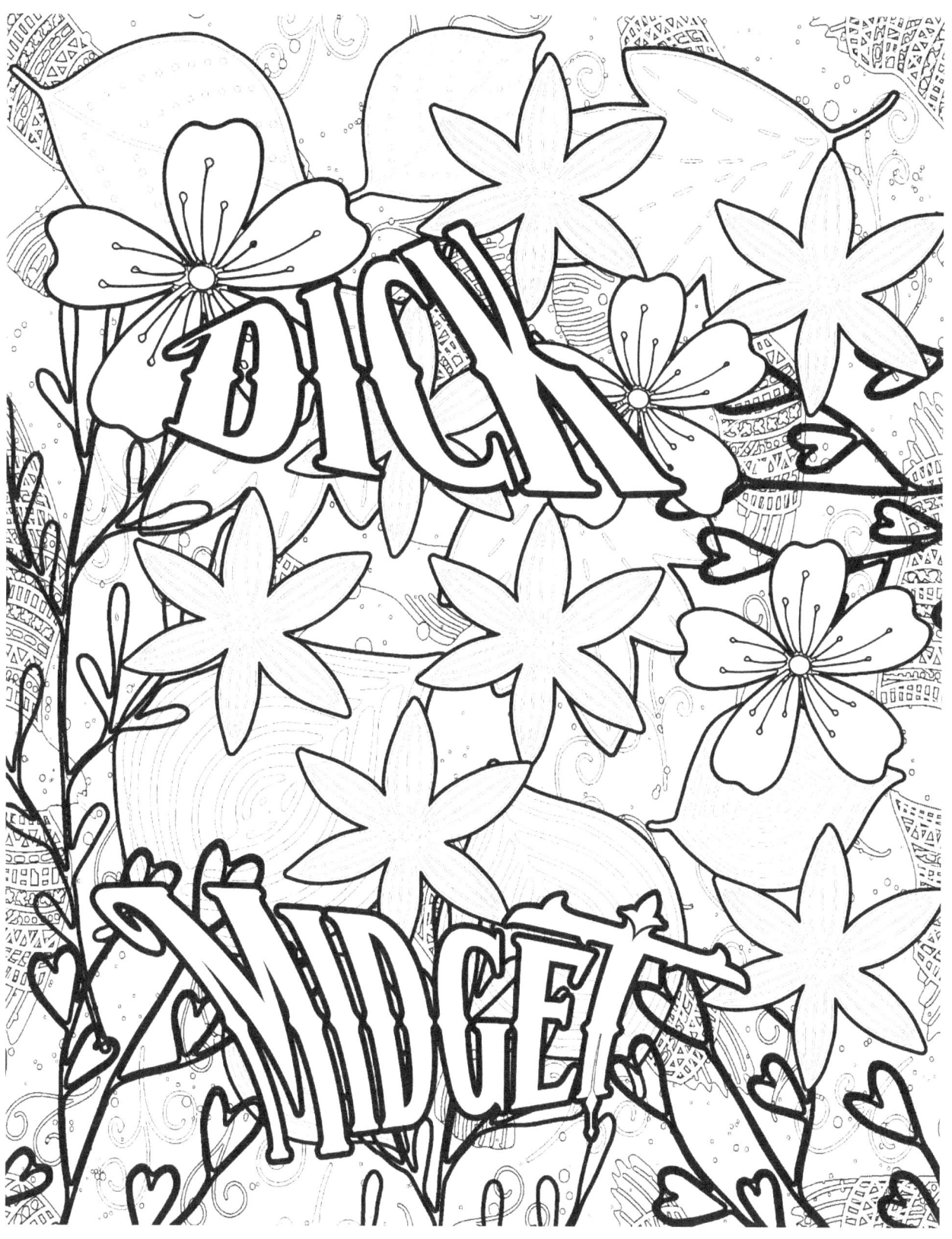

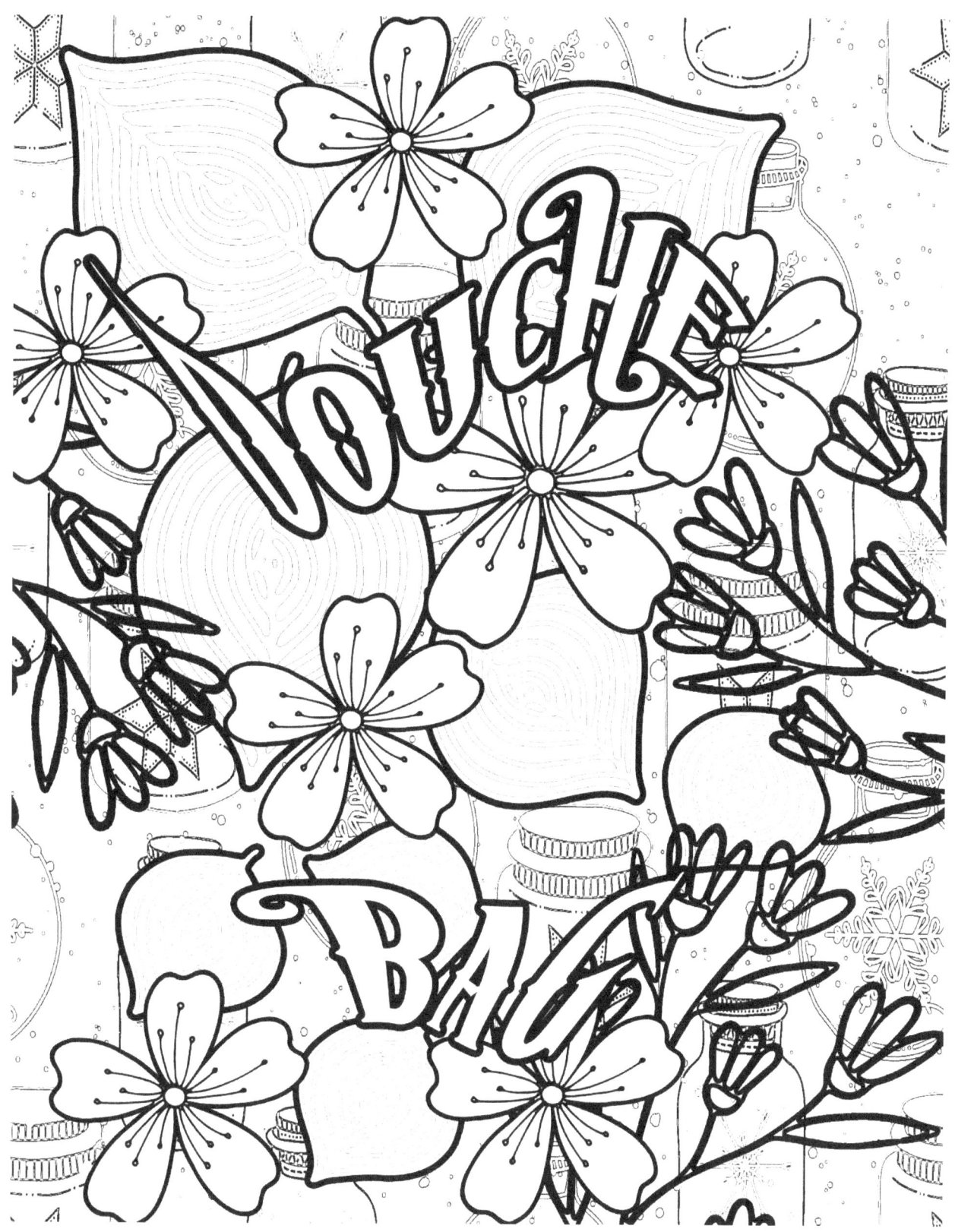

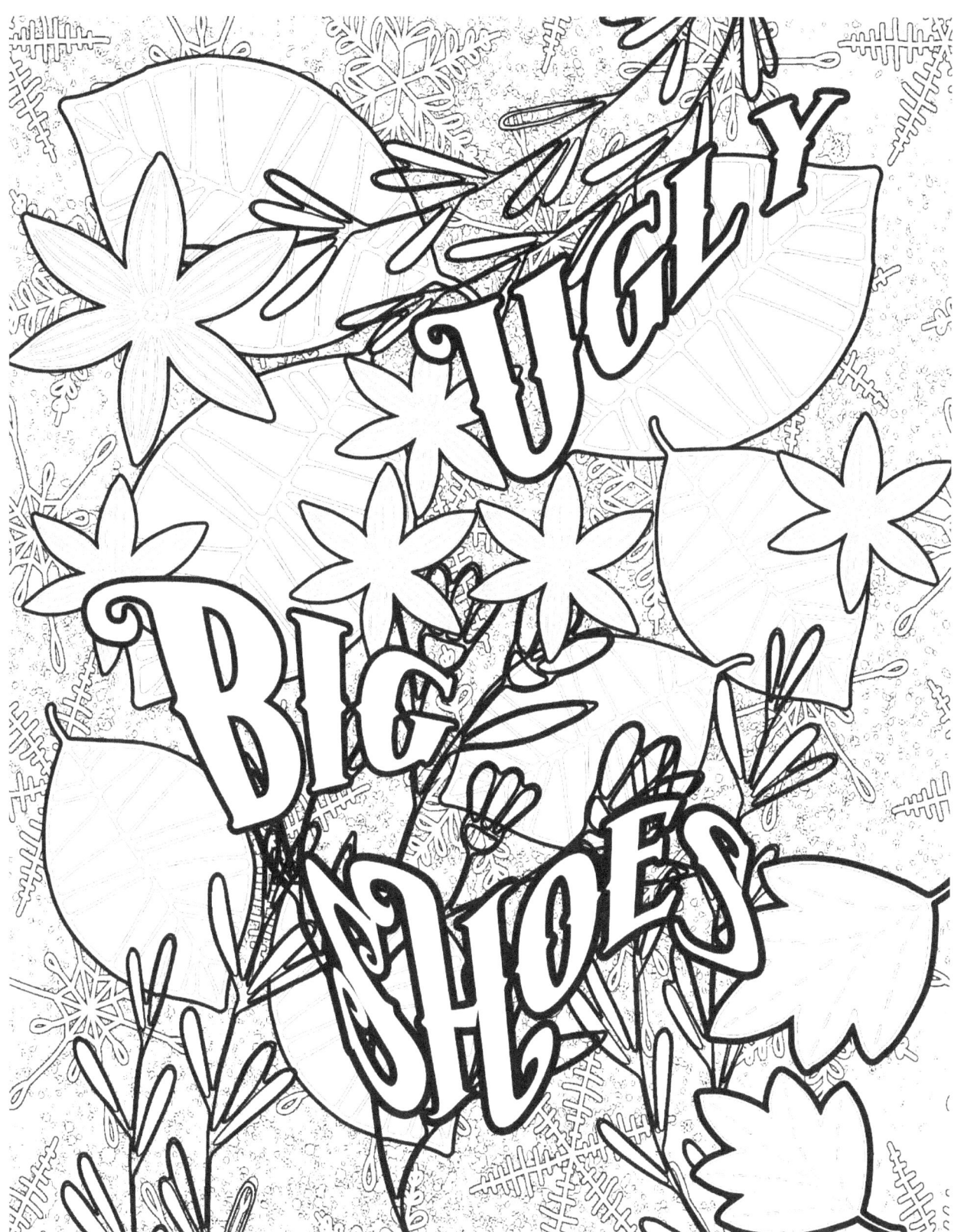

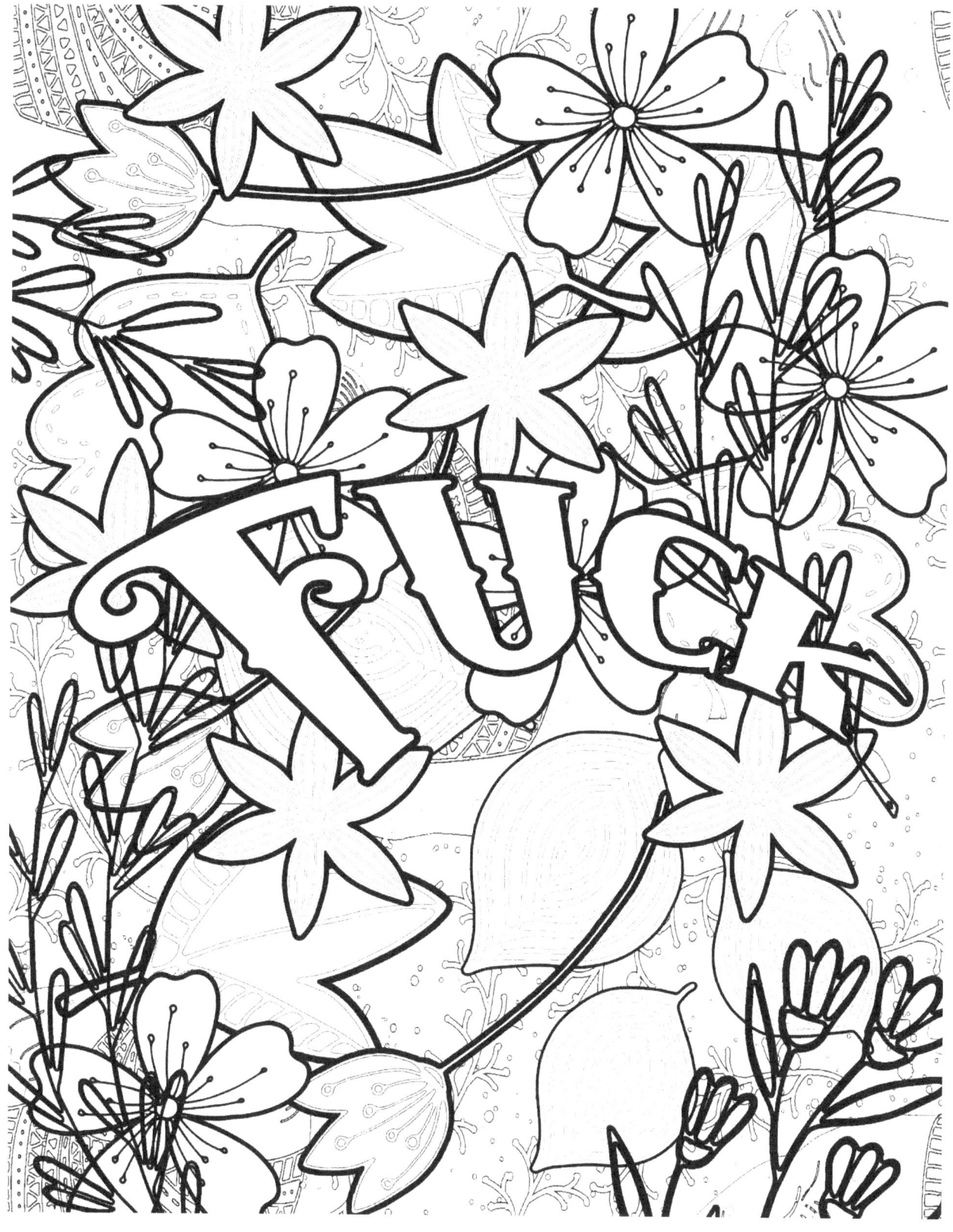

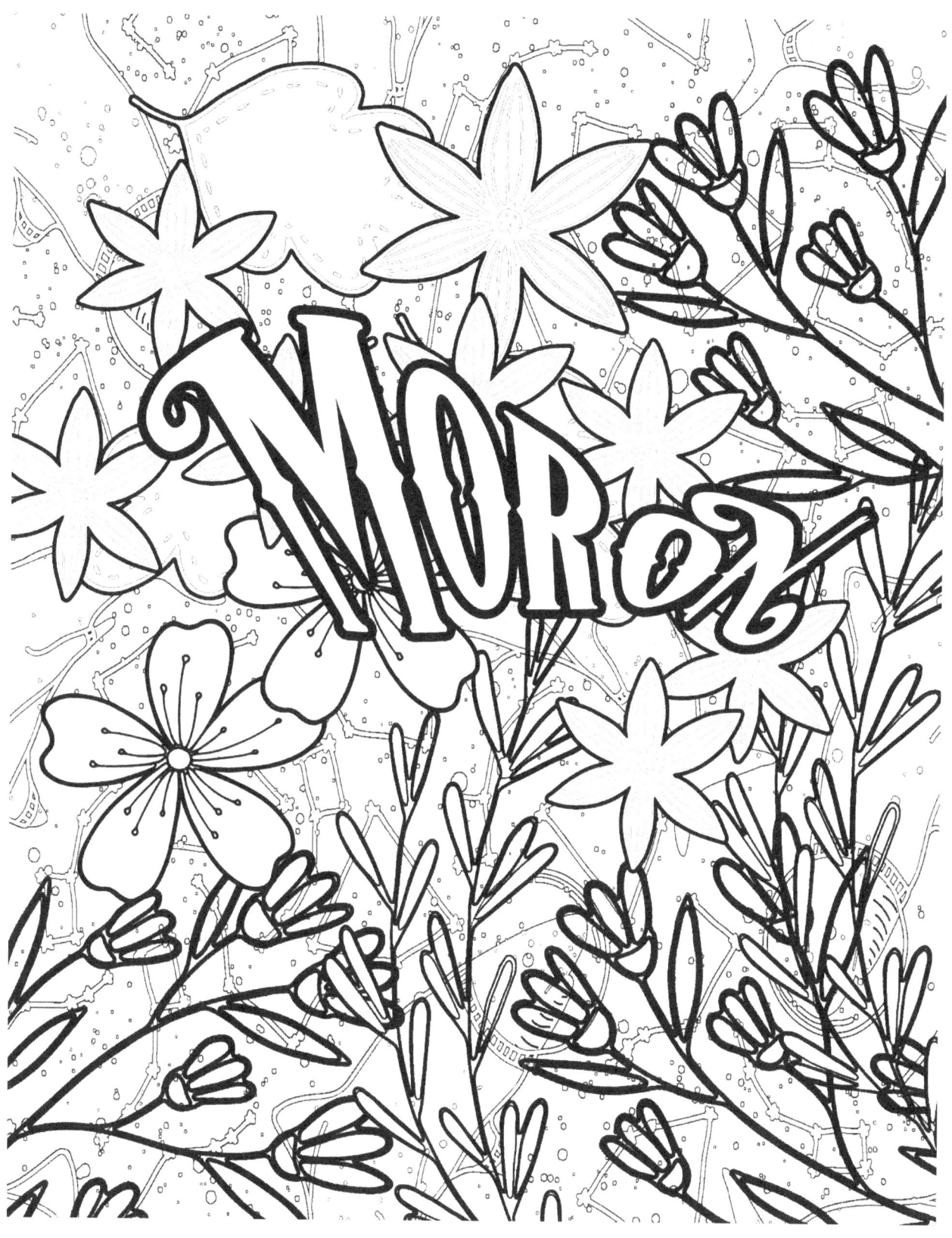

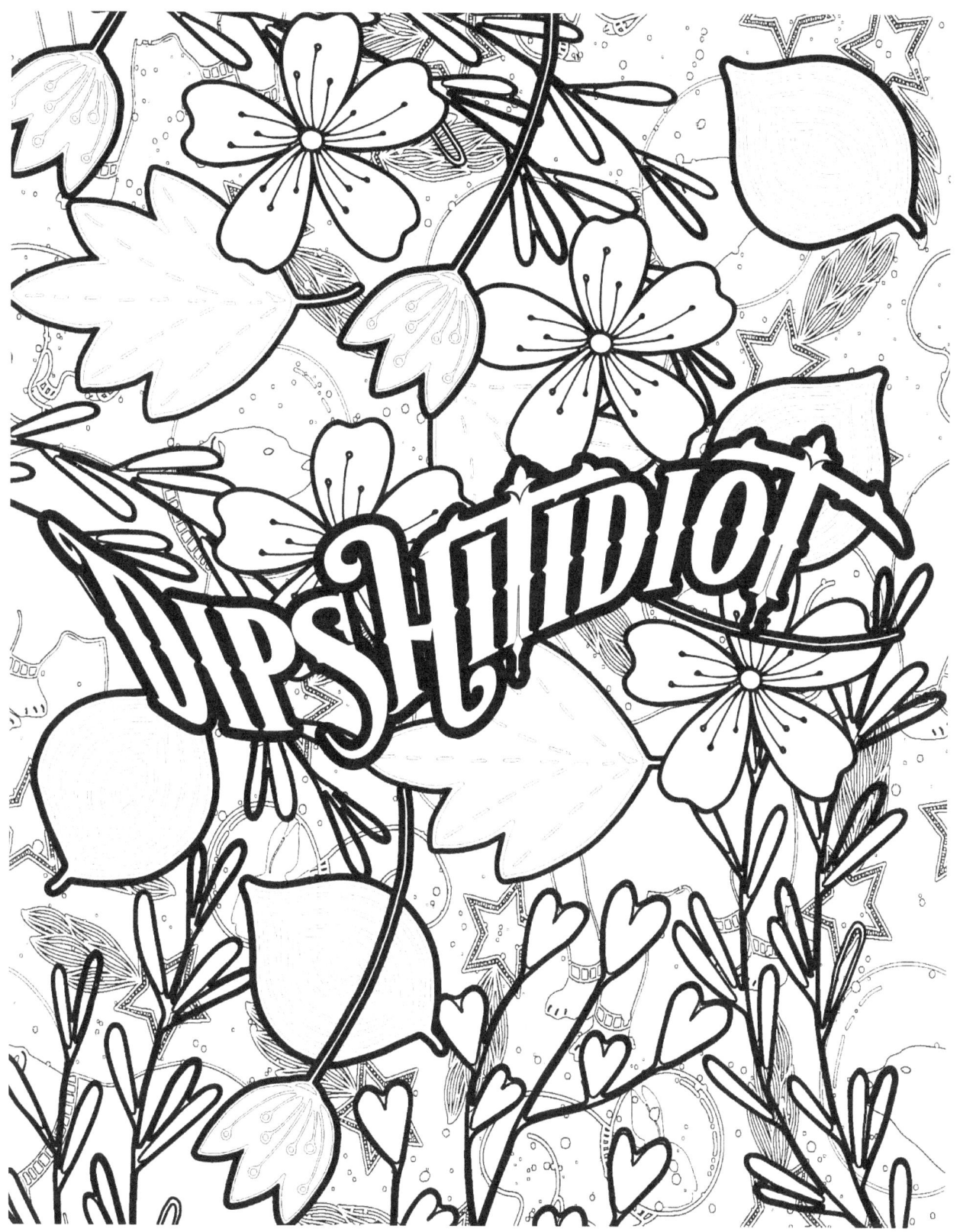

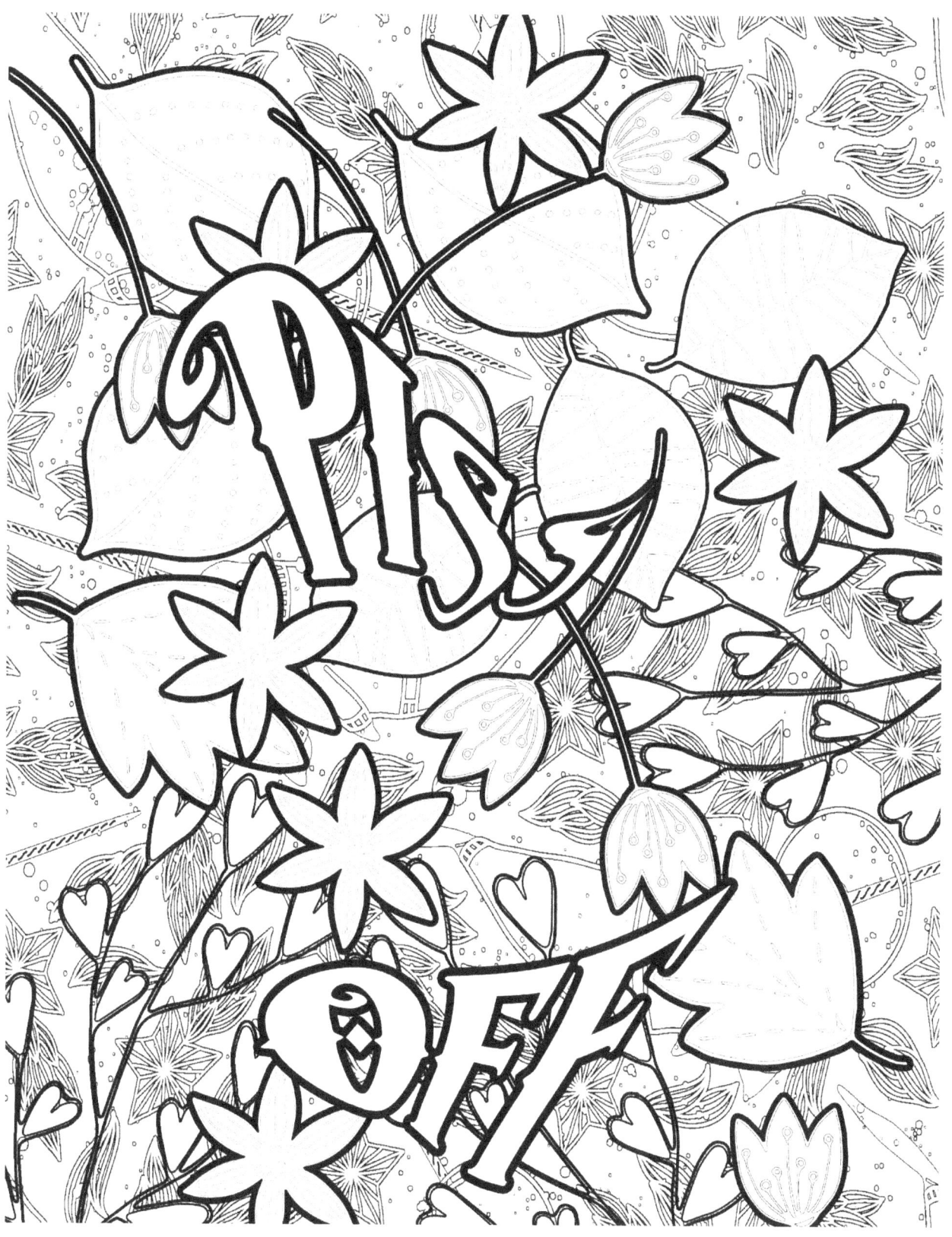

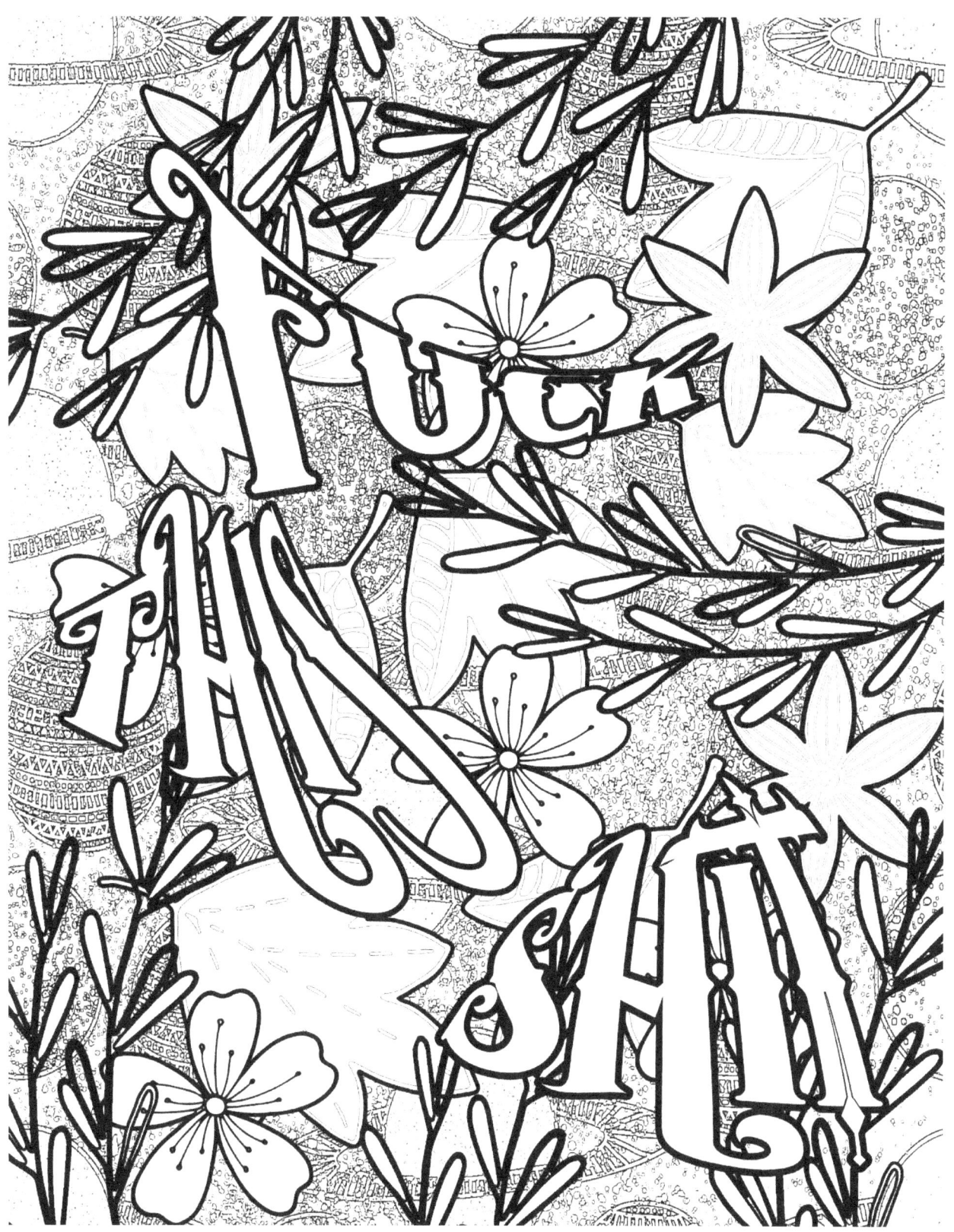

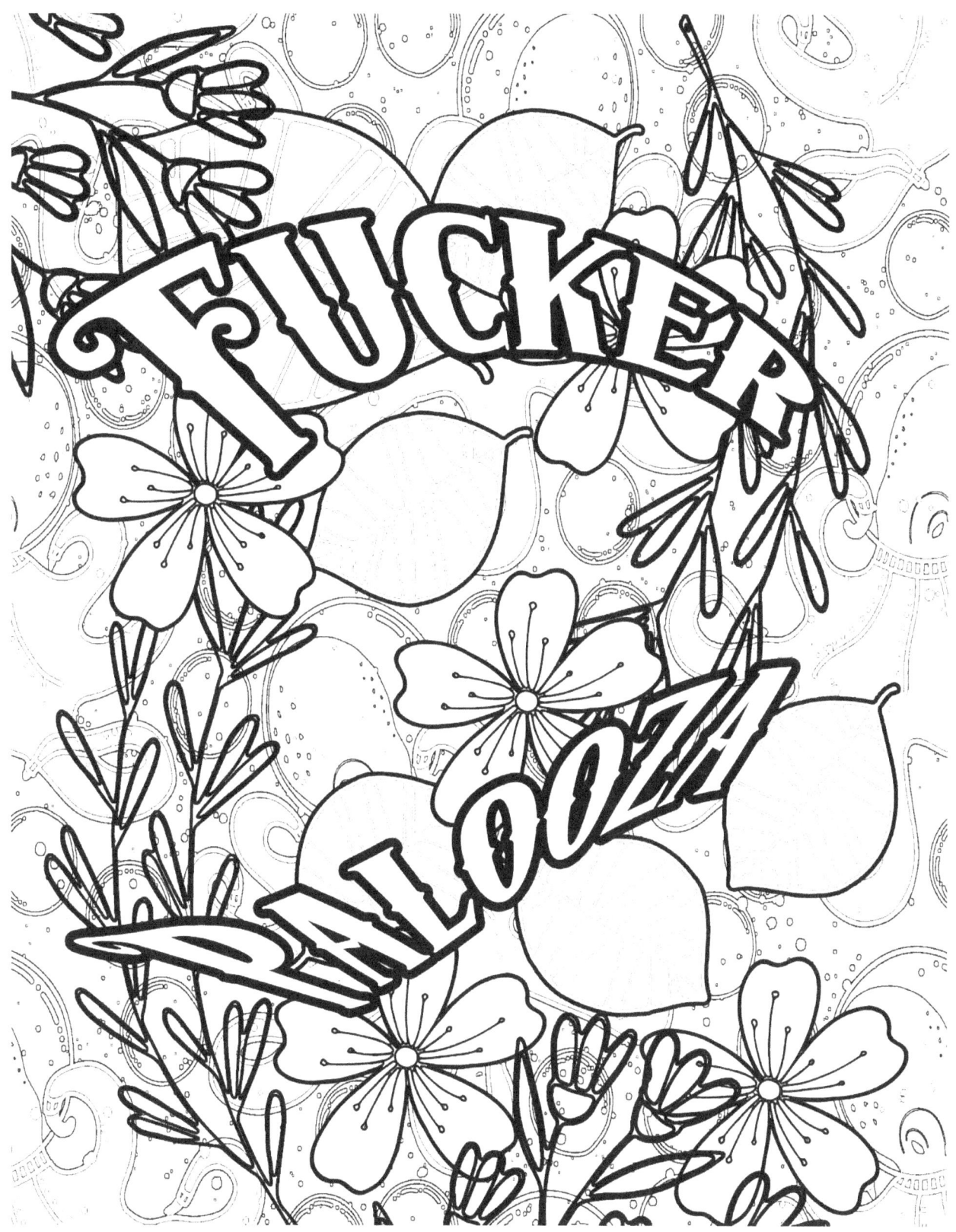

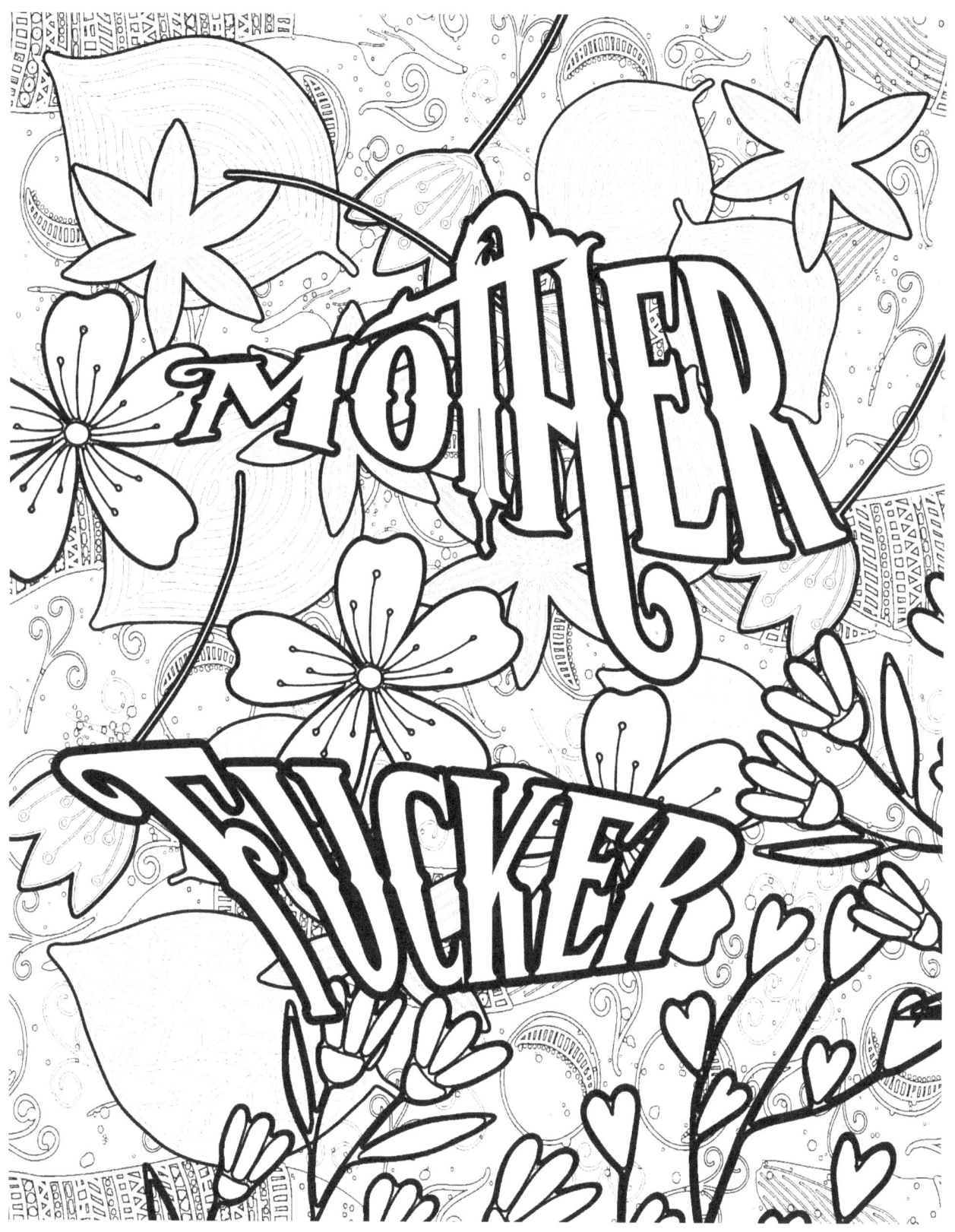

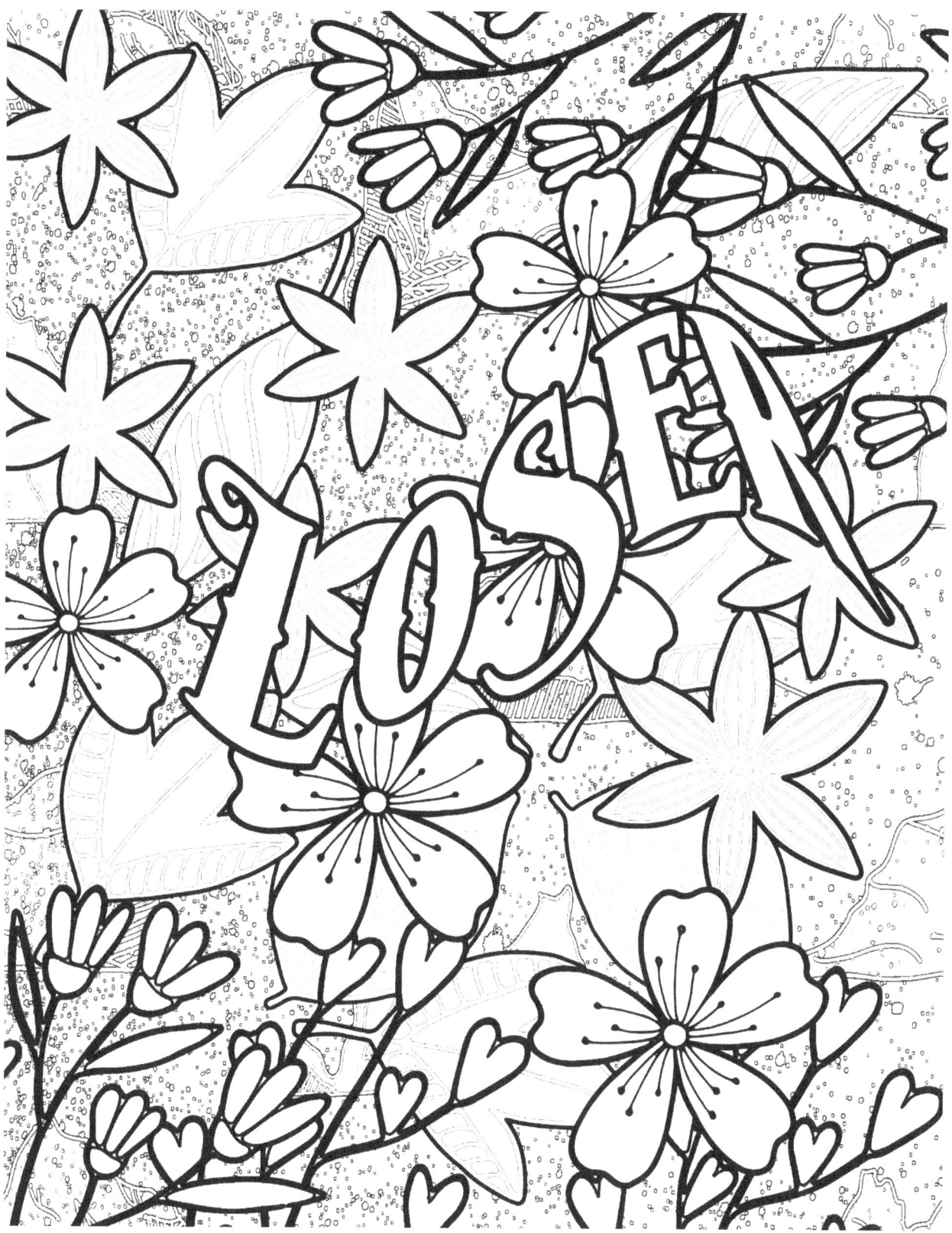

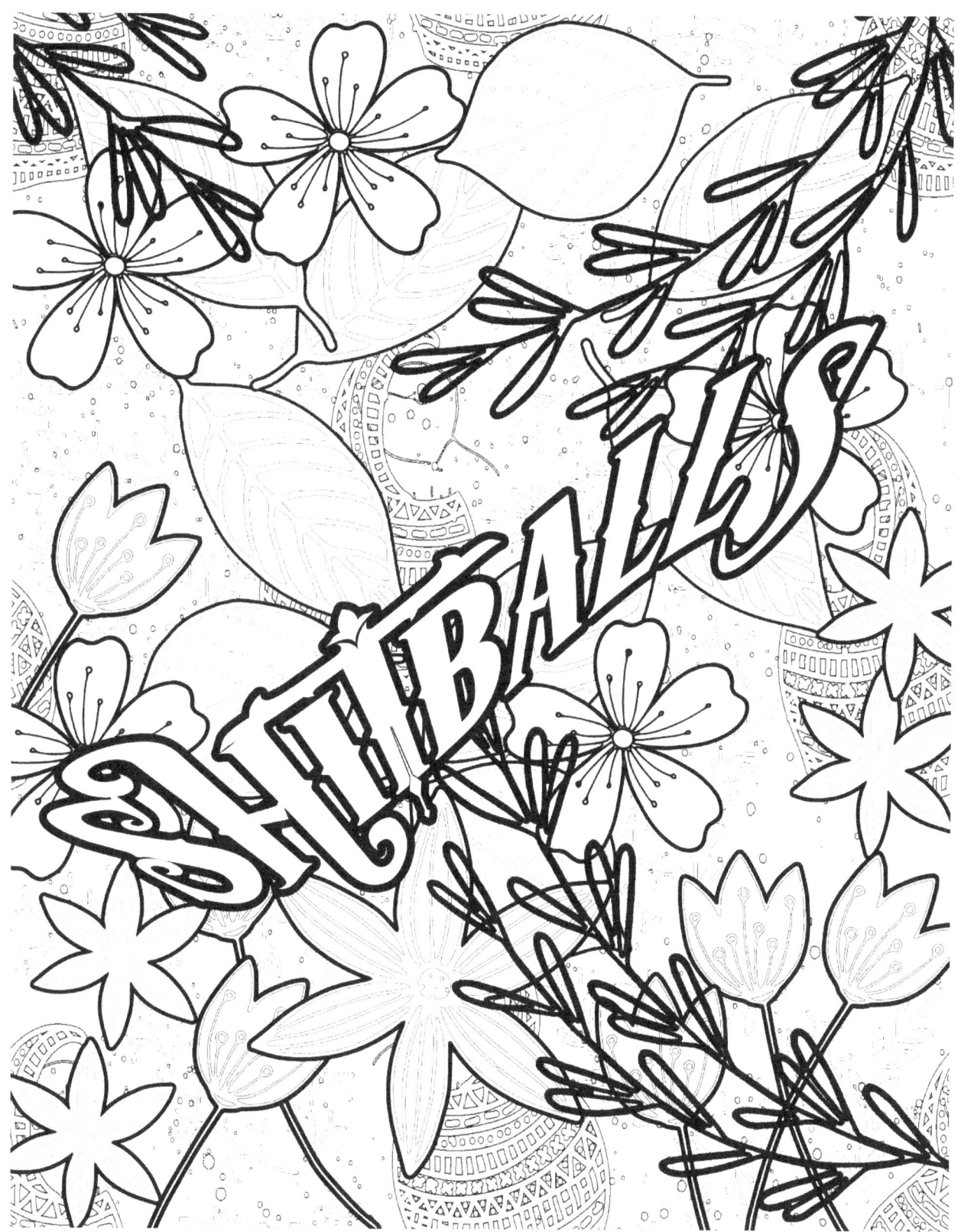

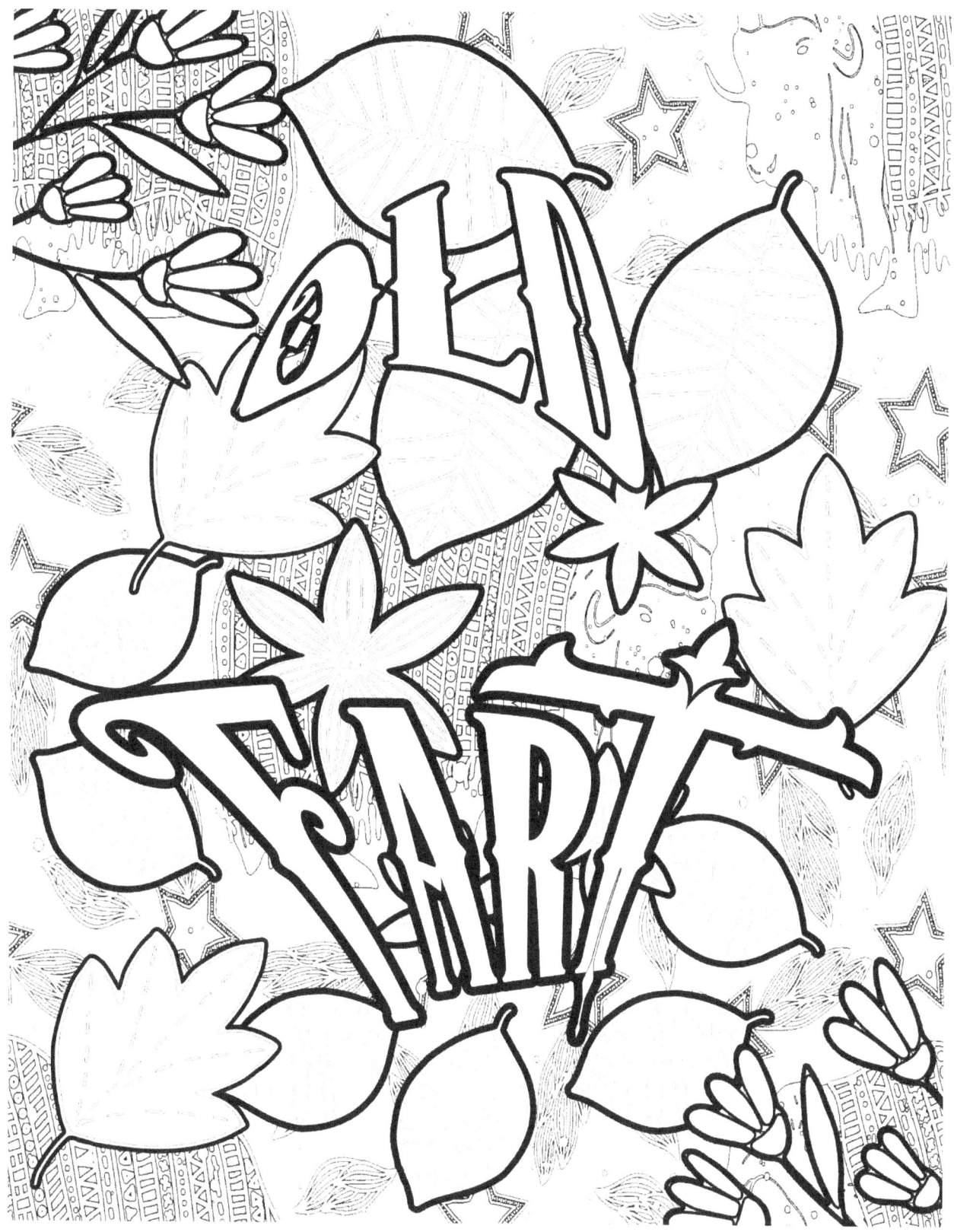

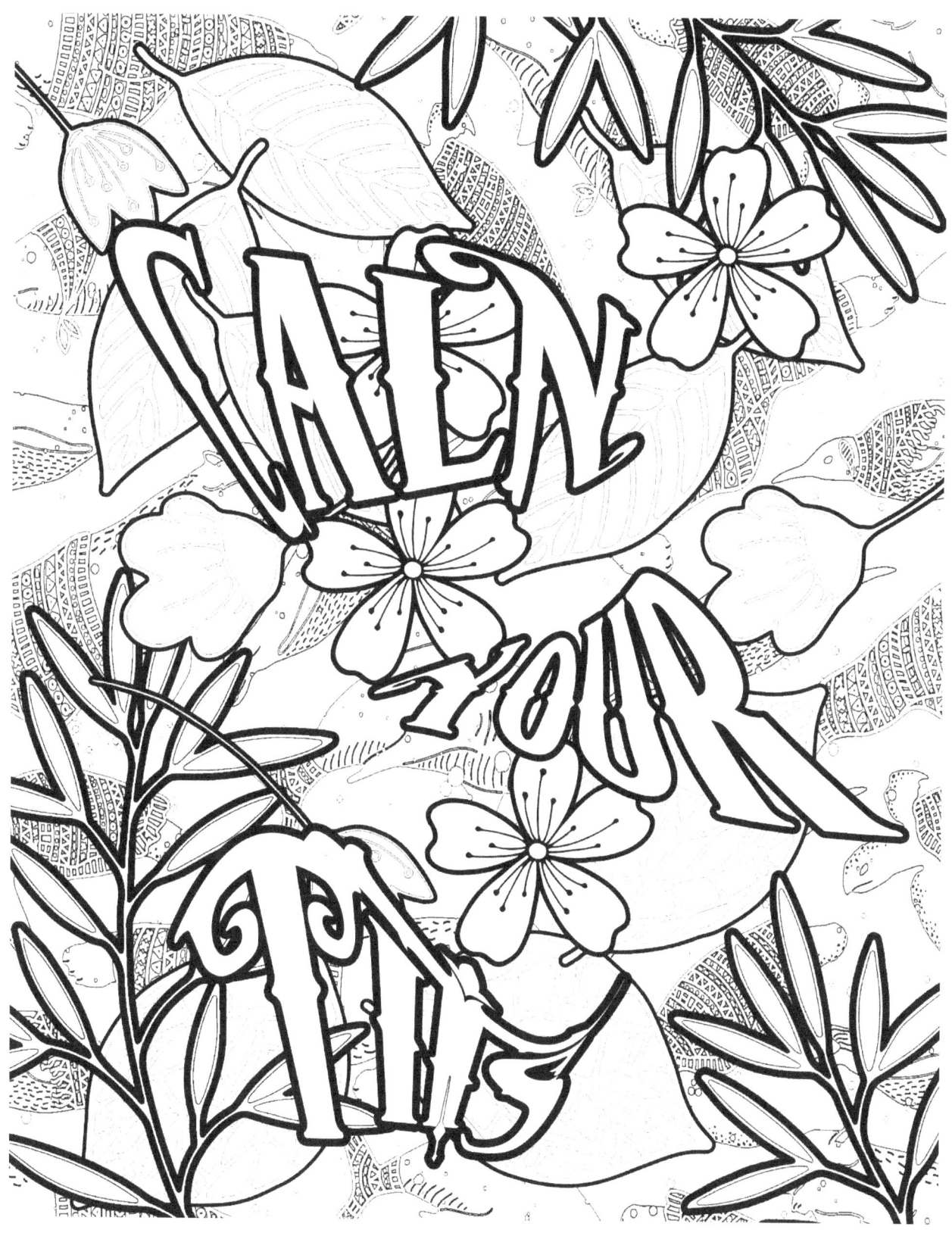

Note

www.ingramcontent.com/pod-product-compliance
Lightning Source LLC
Chambersburg PA
CBHW081122180526
45170CB00008B/2969